Formative assessment in adult literacy, language and numeracy

Jay Derrick, Kathryn Ecclestone
and Judith Gawn

niace

promoting adu

D0273369

© 2009 National Institute of Adult Continuing Education
(England and Wales)

21 De Montfort Street
Leicester LE1 7GE

Company registration no. 2603322

Charity registration no. 1002775

NIACE has a broad remit to promote lifelong learning opportunities for adults.
NIACE works to develop increased participation in education and training,
particularly for those who do not have easy access because of class, gender, age,
race, language and culture, learning difficulties or disabilities, or insufficient
financial resources.

For a full catalogue of all NIACE's publications visit

http://shop.niace.org.uk/

Cataloguing in Publications Data
A CIP record for this title is available from the British Library

ISBN 978-1-86201-438-1

Designed and typeset by Book Production Services

Printed in England by Page Brothers, Norwich

Contents

Introduction

This booklet aims to provide practical ideas for teachers of adult literacy, language and numeracy (ALLN) in their day-to-day work of lesson preparation, teaching and assessment. It is relevant for working with students at all levels and in different contexts. It is not an instruction manual or a primer, and it certainly isn't any kind of magic fix for solving all the problems teachers face.

Instead, it argues for a focus on basic principles of teaching and learning in adult education: student-centred learning, teaching and assessment that put the goal of student autonomy at the heart of the process. It embodies approaches that treat adult students as serious, experienced and competent people who are active and engaged, rather than 'vulnerable' or 'fragile' and passive recipients of this or that prescribed curriculum. This view presents teaching and learning as primarily focused on real-life tasks and practices, where the passing of tests whose main purpose is not to support learning, but to provide evidence for funding and quality assurance, is secondary.

The ideas in the booklet, and the research they are based on, are gathered under the term 'formative assessment'. Although this term can be confusing and even misleading, it is used here because a great deal of previous research uses it, and because it is now cropping up in policy documents and other published documents aimed at improving the quality of teaching. A key aim of this booklet is to clarify what formative assessment is and what it isn't, though its main purpose, as already stated, is to help support the work of teachers in classrooms.

What formative assessment is

Formative assessment is an approach to planning and implementing teaching and learning methods based on fundamental principles of learning and on recent research on effective practice. There is currently no watertight definition of formative assessment. It is often described as 'assessment *for* learning' as distinct from 'assessment *of* learning':

> *Assessment for learning is any assessment for which the first priority in its design and practice is to serve the purpose of promoting students' learning. It thus differs from assessment designed primarily to serve the purposes of accountability, or of ranking, or of certifying competence. An assessment activity can help learning if it provides information to be used as feedback, by teachers, and by their students, in assessing themselves and each other, to modify the teaching and learning activities in which they are engaged. Such assessment becomes 'formative assessment' when the evidence is actually used to adapt the teaching work to meet learning needs*

> (Black *et al.*, 2002).

A widely quoted and influential idea about formative assessment comes from Roy Sadler who defines it as follows:

> *In assessment for learning, the learner's task is to close the gap between the present state of understanding and the learning goal. Self-assessment is essential if the learner is to do this. The teacher's role is to communicate appropriate goals and promote self-assessment as pupils work towards the goals. Feedback in the classroom should operate from teacher to pupils and from pupils to teacher*

> (Sadler, 1989).

However, this should not imply a one-way route of feedback from teacher to student: feedback from a student about his or her own performance, or to other students about their performance (self and peer assessment) are widely seen as integral to effective formative assessment. Some researchers observe that even when feedback from teachers is regular, detailed and helpful, students fail to improve: As Sadler argues:

> *For students to be able to improve, they must develop the capacity to monitor the quality of their own work during actual production. This in turn requires that students possess an appreciation of what high quality work is, that they have the evaluative skill necessary for them to compare with some objectivity the quality of what they are producing in relation to the higher standard, and that they develop a store of tactics or moves which can be drawn on to modify their own work*

> (Sadler 1989, p.119)

Formative assessment embedded in everyday teaching

Many teachers equate formative and diagnostic assessment with specific processes and techniques such as creating Individual Learning Plans, reviewing individual progress in tutorials, compiling portfolios of work or marking students' work. Whilst technically part of formative assessment, a focus on specific processes or methods can lead to a narrow, instrumental approach that focuses on 'getting through the targets' and is therefore part of summative assessment. In other words, reviewing progress, carrying out diagnostic assessment etc, can sound formative but, in practice, not be (see, for example, Ecclestone 2010). A more useful and holistic approach is offered by Paul Black who regards feedback as integral to good formative assessment, based on peer- and self-assessment tasks, carefully constructed discussion and dialogue, written and oral feedback on classroom and individual work, and open-ended classroom questioning (Black, 2007). From this perspective, formative assessment is embedded in the teaching of subjects, where cognitive and skills progression in numeracy, literacy or language is the primary purpose. This requires teachers to think about the progression first and then how various methods realise it.

In keeping with the idea that formative assessment is embedded in everyday teaching and learning, Dylan Wiliam argues that teachers need to think about such processes as part of a 'pedagogy of engagement', where they have to make students engage at a higher level cognitively than they want to, or would choose to. This means capitalising on what he calls 'moments of contingency', where learning might go one way or the other. He argues that this does not require a view of what is to be learned, or about what happens when learning takes place, but is crucially a pedagogic focus, a way of informing better teaching decisions and a way of finding new ways to break down complex learning activities into small steps (Wiliam, 2008).

From this perspective, assessment cannot be understood as formative unless evidence from feedback is actually used to adapt teaching and learning activities. This iteration between feedback, whether from students' written work or their answers to classroom or tutorial questions, can be minute-to-minute as teachers and tutors think on their feet and respond to individuals or groups during classroom sessions or tutorials, or more considered as teachers plan new activities and lessons. For Black and colleagues, students' half-correct answers, their mistaken understandings or their wrong answers are essential to the sort of diagnosis that good teachers make to inform their responses and inputs.

A formative assessment approach to teaching and learning is therefore a complex and continuous process of activity, reflection, communication, and evaluation taking place between teacher and students and between the students themselves. The outcomes lead to repeated adaptations and refinements of the activities taking place, with the aim of continuously improving and sustaining learning for all the students.

This concept of formative assessment encapsulates four fundamental assumptions:

1. Teaching and learning is essentially an *iterative* process for both students and teachers, one that is continually adjusted on the basis of new information or ideas. This means that planning cannot just be a mechanical process of deciding in advance what is going to happen and writing it in the form of a lesson plan. It is more a case of planning for possible classroom activities, particularly framing good 'diagnostic' questions and offering opportunities for self and peer assessment, and being able to change these on the basis of what happens.

2. The success of the learning process can only be judged in any meaningful sense by those at the centre of the process, i.e. the teacher and students: they may of course agree that success is defined as the gaining of an externally-validated qualification.

3. Success is often a relative concept: different people can have different ways of thinking about success in learning, just as they may have different purposes for learning, whatever the official reason for having started the course. This aspect of the definition aligns it very well with the context of adult learning in all its great variety of forms, contexts, and purposes.

4. A formative approach avoids being prescriptive, in the sense of saying that 'these are the right things to do' and 'these are the wrong things to do' for teachers and students: it does not say that some activities or materials are essentially formative, and that others cannot ever be used formatively. Rather, it implies that all materials, techniques, tools, and assessment activities (including standardised tests) have the potential to contribute formatively to teaching and learning: how they are used determines how much this potential is realised.

Two practical aspects of formative assessment

Two distinct aspects of formative assessment in teaching and learning are vitally important for students of adult literacy, language and numeracy. The first consists of practices and activities that aim to produce evidence for planning future learning and/or for constructive feedback and review: these might include activities such as assignments, tests, role-play, performances, observations, questioning, etc. It is important to note that these activities can also be used primarily for purposes that are not essentially formative or to support learning, for example to fulfil bureaucratic requirements or to serve the purposes of summative assessment.

Such activities are the main means by which teachers find out and continue revising what needs to be taught and how best to teach it, given the different and developing profiles and personalities of their students. This kind of assessment starts at the beginning of learning programmes, or even before this, and should be continuous throughout the learning programme, so that both teacher and students can regularly update their information about what has been learned and about the developing understanding and motivation of the students, and adjust the teaching plan accordingly, both during the lesson, and from lesson to lesson.

Formative assessment therefore aims to increase the accuracy of teaching and learning activities, and of feedback as students' skills, knowledge, understanding and motivation develop. The key activity is dialogue between the learner and teacher, and the teacher's role is to enable, stimulate and develop this dialogue through such means as constructive and open-ended questioning, and through generating an atmosphere in which students can think and talk about what they are learning and understanding.

Secondly, formative assessment can take the form of learning activities which aim to develop the autonomy of students by enabling them to practise relevant skills and knowledge in real-life contexts, and particularly in assessing their performance and those of others, in those contexts. This type of assessment activity adds a critical dimension to learning itself, as something which, *when practised by students themselves*, adds to the acquisition of knowledge and skills and to students' development and exercise of judgement about performance, appropriateness, accuracy, authenticity, and beauty. A focus on autonomy, on successful performance not just in formal educational contexts, but outside in the real world, is therefore essential for improvement and the sustainability of knowledge and understanding.

The aims of this booklet

This booklet responds to four findings from recent research, all of which are particularly relevant to the work of adult literacy, language and numeracy teachers.

- *First*, formative assessment approaches are strongly correlated with successful and sustainable learning (Black and Wiliam, 1998a).

- *Second*, positive benefits of formative approaches are even

7

more marked for less confident students, and those with unsuccessful or negative previous experience of learning (Harlen and Deakin Crick, 2002).

- *Third*, the present context for adult literacy, numeracy and language learning is highly pressured for both students and teachers, as a result of the high political profile given to the work in recent years, and of the political importance attached to easily-measurable and short term outcomes of learning, as key elements of funding and inspection systems (Derrick, Merrifield and Ecclestone, 2007).

- *Fourth*, following the adoption and incorporation of the term 'formative assessment' into numerous recent policy initiatives, often inconsistently and in ways unfounded in research, teachers and provider organisations are confused about its meaning and how to put a formative assessment approach into practice (Derrick, Gawn and Ecclestone, 2008).

For all these reasons, we hope that a short guide to the research evidence for using formative assessment approaches, and what this might mean in practice, is both timely and useful to adult literacy, language and numeracy teachers. Similar recent publications about formative assessment in different subjects in schools have been welcomed by teachers, and teacher responses at professional development sessions led in various post-16 contexts by the authors over the past two years have also been highly positive and enthusiastic.

This booklet does not offer comprehensive or prescriptive guidance for teachers in all situations, and still less should it be seen as a manual. Rather, it is a 'rough guide' to formative practice in adult literacy, language and numeracy classes. The formative assessment approach to teaching and learning cannot be reduced to a list of handy tips and techniques, to be applied at one or more pre-determined 'stages' in the learning cycle. This conception, found in some recent published resource guides for teachers (for example, see QIA, 2008a), ignores the need to create a learning culture within the classroom that enables each student to become an independent and effective learner. This approach also undermines the professional role of the teacher in assessing the needs and preferences of individual students and organising activities and programmes to meet them as responsively and appropriately as possible. This is far too complex a task to be meaningfully reduced to a simple recipe.

Barriers to understanding and using formative assessment in adult education

Our research has identified significant barriers to enabling teachers to use formative assessment in ways that enhance genuine learning as opposed to getting students and teachers through tests and targets.

First, testing systems can make it harder for teachers and providers to focus on the actual needs of students, and encourage them to reflect less on their practice than on their 'results profile' each term, which can lead to 'teaching to the test'. There is powerful evidence that if teachers and organisations focus strongly on this type of measure of success, they are highly unlikely to use genuine formative assessment approaches (Black and Wiliam, 1998a; Torrance *et al.*, 2005). The present system's overemphasis on quick, easily-measurable achievements may inhibit the development of the learner's autonomy and actually undermine 'sustainable' learning (Boud, 2000). Teachers who are aware of this see themselves as having to work 'against' the system to support their students' real needs (Derrick, Gawn and Ecclestone, 2008; Looney, 2008).

Second, the way in which the concept of formative assessment has been incorporated recently into policy initiatives such as *Skills for Life* is a good example of the paradox at the heart of attempts to formulate 'best practice' in teaching and learning and then require all teachers to follow it. In contrast, teaching is a highly complex activity where what works well in one situation may well fail in another, and where the focus shifts continually as students develop their skills, knowledge and their attitudes to learning. It follows from this that over-prescriptive injunctions about 'best practice' often has the effect of deskilling teachers, encouraging them to rely too much on codified, systematised frameworks that dictate their working practices. Numerous research studies on changing assessment practice show that the need for teachers to hone and update and extend their professional expertise cannot be reduced to a technical process of assimilating 'best practice' (see for example Black *et al.*, 2003; Ecclestone, 2010; Fielding *et al.*, 2005; Pickering, 2007). This paradox is producing a tension between what teachers are at present required to do to 'prove' that they are working effectively, and what they perceive to be the real needs of students. This issue is discussed in more detail at the end of section 1.

Third, students bring powerful images of 'good' teaching, learning and assessment from their previous experiences, and these exert strong influences over their expectations, attitudes and responses and over what they think teachers should do in the classroom. Teachers therefore need a strong sense of their own values and beliefs, a good subject knowledge base and a repertoire of techniques that they can use and adapt. They also need to judge when to support and when to challenge their students, and when to try to change features of the 'learning cultures' of each group and classroom that might encourage students to stay in a comfort zone or to resist particular approaches to learning and assessment.

Fourth, many teachers and some (but by no means all) students have a tendency to think of adults doing literacy, language or numeracy as 'fragile' or 'vulnerable' or as having irredeemably damaging experiences of formal schooling. These images, or stereotypes, can hinder teachers from challenge that pushes or encourages students out of comfort zones. This should not suggest that teachers do not need to be sensitive to particular students' experiences, responses or barriers, but, instead, that such images need to be taken account of in planning formative assessment and other teaching-related activities.

The organisation of this guide

There are two main sections of the booklet. In the first section, after a brief initial discussion of what formative assessment is not, we look in turn at five broad aspects of formative assessment that were found in the research to be important in raising achievement and at the same time supporting sustainable learning:

- students examining and discussing learning goals and success criteria;

- planning and managing effective classroom discussions, questions and tasks that produce evidence that learning has taken place;

- providing constructive feedback;

- collaborative learning activities based on real-life problems and situations relevant to all the students;

- developing learner autonomy, motivation and confidence through peer and self-assessment activities.

These aspects of formative assessment are closely linked, even though they will be discussed separately. For example, assessment by students of their own or others' work requires an understanding of success criteria; and constructive

11

feedback will not help students if they do not see the relevance of the tasks they have been carrying out. In fact it will become clear that the different aspects overlap and are interlinked in all sorts of ways.

In this section we emphasise the commonalities between approaches to the teaching of adult literacy, numeracy and ESOL, rather than the differences. Of course there are important distinctions in the way the approaches advocated here will be put into practice in teaching and learning in the different subjects. Some of these will be evident in the second section, where we look at specific examples of these approaches in practice. Our belief, however, is that there are things in common about how teachers work well, whatever their subject, and whoever their students, and it is these we are most concerned about here.

The second main section of the book provides very brief examples of the kind of classroom activity that might exemplify formative approaches relevant to literacy, language and numeracy. The final section contains a brief presentation of a formative approach to Continuing Professional Development for ALLN teachers, as well as a glossary, a list of references, and sources of further information and support.

Very little that is discussed here will be entirely new to experienced ALLN teachers. The booklet's main aim is to encourage teachers to develop and exercise their professional skills and judgement in the best interests of students, to unpack the familiar adult education mantra 'student-centred learning', and illuminate what this means in terms of actual classroom practice and preparation, and finally to urge teachers to use these approaches more often in their teaching, and more systematically, than they may have done so far, and to challenge the barriers that prevent them from doing this. The research evidence backs these aims.

Section 1

What formative assessment is not

There is widespread confusion and disagreement at the level of official specifications, practical guidelines and academic research about the meanings and purposes of formative and summative assessment, and the learning activities through which they are carried out. Teachers need to develop their understanding of both formative and summative assessment to avoid the danger of formative assessment activities merely serving the purposes of accountability and certification rather than supporting deeper, sustainable learning.

The highly-prescriptive nature of the *Skills for Life* initiative aggravates this confusion by creating tension in many teachers' minds about what is expected of them:

> *Different traditions, political pressures for targets and professional confusion and disagreement about the purposes of formative assessment are creating tensions between the spirit of formative assessment as a way of engaging learners deeply with their learning in order to develop critical and cognitive autonomy, and the letter of formative assessment that often uses the language of individual empowerment towards the narrow transmission of pre-defined learning targets*

> (*Davies and Ecclestone, 2007*).

In the 'letter' of formative assessment, classroom activities that *look* like formative assessment are less concerned with developing genuine understanding and motivation to go further and deeper in learning. Rather, they are concerned with either the formal recording of achievements or with the teacher carrying out activities that look like formative assessment because that is what they feel is expected of them.

'Formative assessment is continuous assessment'

The most common misunderstanding is that coursework assessment, such as assignments at the end of modules or units, or interim tests, are essentially formative, because they take place throughout the course, or halfway through it, rather than at the end. Rather than being formative, the primary purpose of such assessments is to provide evidence for certification, which is a summative purpose. Coursework assignments or interim tests can be used formatively if they are followed by feedback to help the students improve their work. The critical issue here is what is done with the outcomes of assignments and tests: if teachers use them as sources of evidence which lead to feedback and adaptations in planning lessons, they can be formative as well as summative because they develop learning and understanding as well as providing evidence for certification.

'Formative assessment is a particular stage in a learning cycle'

Rather than being at a point somewhere between initial diagnostic assessment and summative assessment, any element of the learning cycle has the potential to be more or less formative, depending on how it is carried out by the teacher and what its purpose is.

'Formative assessment is a set of particular techniques'

Methods or techniques can be formative or summative, depending on how and why they are used. Students marking their own work, or teachers offering oral and written feedback on their performance, may be examples of self-assessment and feedback, but they are not formative unless such methods enhance students' understanding of their strengths and weaknesses and how to improve their understanding. Similarly, questioning to 'check learning' (in the ubiquitous phrase) is not formative unless it gives students a chance to try out answers and develop their understanding, and unless it enables teachers to detect half understandings or misunderstandings and then to build on those to develop better understanding.

'Formative assessment is setting targets and tracking students' progress towards them'

Activities for diagnosing starting points, negotiating or setting targets and reviewing progress towards them can involve students in little more than a mechanistic, and bureaucratic process of tracking, checking and 'signing off' summative targets with no genuine insight or engagement by students.

Activities to encourage formative assessment

Students examining and discussing learning goals and success criteria

If the acquisition of skills and knowledge is to be sustained and used effectively, students need to understand why and how what they are learning connects with what they already know and with the activities they engage in every day (for example, see Appleby, 2008). This involves students addressing the following questions.

- What is it that I really want to be able to do?

- How well am I doing these things at the moment?

- How can I improve the way I am doing these things at the moment?

- How will I know when I have learned to do them well enough?

Research shows that one reason many adults have problems with literacy, language and numeracy is that there was a 'mismatch' or even conflict between their practices at home and what they were being taught in school (Reder, 1994). The alternative is to help students to see and understand the strengths and limitations of their existing practices (Appleby and Barton, 2008), and to envision how they might develop their skills to achieve new goals; in short, to see as clearly as possible the gap between where they are and where they want to be. This demands a focus not just on the skills and practices involved (for example, calculating percentages, using tenses or spelling correctly), but also an understanding of what 'success' means in using these activities – depending on the context, the other people involved, or whether it is being formally measured in any way. This understanding requires practice in self-assessment:

> *Pupils can only assess themselves when they have a sufficiently clear picture of the targets that their learning is meant to attain… what this amounts to is that self-assessment by pupils, far from being a luxury, is in fact an essential component of formative assessment*

> (Black and Wiliam, 1998b).

We discuss self-assessment activities later in this section. Here we are focusing on the question of what it means to be successful in a particular task or activity, as an essential element of learning. Encouraging students to develop, discuss and evaluate their own assessment criteria and assessment materials, as well as collectively drafting and evaluating 'perfect' answers, will help them understand both 'official' and 'unofficial' assessment criteria. This enables them not only to develop their learning but also see the value of whatever formal external assessment they are undergoing. This applies equally to students at lower levels, though careful preparation is needed if it is to be effective, for example, for ESOL students at Entry 1, as one of the case studies given in the next section shows. There is evidence that this kind of activity can improve 'pass rates', even though its focus is not directly on the knowledge content of the assessment concerned. This means that spending time on these types of activities should not be seen as taking time away from 'coverage' of the official content of the course, but as a key part of preparing students for both the final assessment and for the effective use of the skills they are learning afterwards in real-life situations.

It follows that discussing and clarifying learning goals is also a vital part of effective learning and understanding. Much has been written recently about Individual Learning Plans as a focus for setting 'targets for learning' (see for example Hamilton, 2009). Given the widespread misunderstanding discussed above, we believe that it is the way these plans are used that makes the difference between their summative and formative uses, and whether they contribute to effective learning or are no more than a way of recording targets as part of a bureaucratic requirement.

KEY POINTS

- Students need to learn not just subject knowledge and skills, but how to assess their use of them in real-life situations.

- Classroom activities that support this include discussion and design of appropriate assessment criteria, and students constructively assessing their own work and that of others.

- With careful preparation, students at all levels can take part in these activities.

- These activities are most useful and effective when they are integrated fully into the learning programme.

Planning and managing effective classroom discussions, questions and tasks that produce evidence of learning

Purposeful two-way communication about the process and content of learning is the medium through which genuine understanding and the acquisition of skills and knowledge takes place. A focus on planning teaching and learning activities as a dialogue between teachers and students, and between students, is effective if dialogue is open-ended and exploratory rather than a series of routine exchanges. The focus of this dialogue can be about how people approach problems, and evaluate their learning, as well as how they acquire and develop subject knowledge and understand the formal assessment criteria.

Discussions, conversations, questions and even arguments in the classroom enable students to practise and use skills and knowledge, evaluate their practice, and check their understanding. They are also a key means through which the teacher gains knowledge about the motivations, attitudes and responses of individual students, about what students know already, and of what they seem to have learned so far. Teachers need to keep checking their assessments so that they can plan effectively for the short, medium and long term.

Two factors are critical to supporting this kind of classroom talk: teachers need to exemplify a relaxed but purposeful dialogic model of communication, and to create an atmosphere that allows students to ask questions, to be willing to work collaboratively, to risk making mistakes and, crucially, to articulate the things they don't understand or want to know more about. Many ALLN students are initially very nervous about doing any of these three things, and resistant to them.

Teachers have to find ways to counter these responses and to give students the confidence needed since, without them, they are teaching 'in the dark' by intuition, rather than on the basis of knowledge of their students. It is especially important for students to learn the value of errors and mistakes in developing their knowledge and understanding. While a good physical environment is important, the main way to develop confidence is through the communicative behaviour of teachers through the ways in which they encourage students to relate to and communicate with one another, they ways in which they ask questions of and respond to students, the extent to which they set up peer discussions and group activities, and the way they give verbal and written feedback.

This has complex implications for teachers' planning because it requires students to see that they can influence what happens during lessons, where the expertise and activities of the teacher builds on their responses. On the other hand, teachers also need to plan ahead. Yet, the ability to adapt or even abandon a rigid plan is supported by American research which emphasises the importance of being able to take advantage of unexpected developments during a class, described as 'going with the teachable moment' (Condelli *et al.*, 2003). Adult LLN students are more likely to persist in tackling difficult tasks and ideas if they can see that teachers adapt their teaching in the light of their understanding of what students need (QIA, 2008b).

One way of thinking about this is that teachers foster both the spirit and procedures of a 'joint enquiry' through which students can construct shared meanings from the necessarily different frames of reference which each of them brings to a particular task. Indeed, research suggests that arguments between students can, as part of a carefully structured process, be a powerful means of learning and developing motivation (see for example Cooke and Roberts, 2007; Swan, 2006).

Some suggestions for fostering dialogue based on disagreement for the purposes of developing confidence and language skills in ESOL classes are given by Cooke and Roberts (2007). They could be adapted for literacy and numeracy students, and include:

- If a discussion naturally arises, allow space within the lesson for it to develop. Listen to students to find out their opinions and what they are interested in discussing. Encourage them to talk about current affairs and issues that arise in the international, national and local news.

- Set up a discussion activity which you predict will cause a divergence of opinion amongst the learners. This might come from a reading or listening text from existing materials or from newspapers, magazines, TV or radio. You could ask learners to provide their own topics, or set up formal debates. Decide on the amount of planning time students might need to decide on their opinions and think of counter-arguments.

- Record your learners having a discussion. Transcribe parts of it and discuss their rhetorical styles.

- Give learners arguments to analyse from other sources. Try to get examples of people employing different rhetorical styles.

(Adapted slightly from Cooke and Roberts, 2007.)

In the context of numeracy, the discussions might be about mathematical topics in the news, such as bonuses and pay rates of different workers, or about the best practical approaches to dealing with everyday tasks such as budgeting.

Developing a repertoire of questioning techniques, and sharing ideas with colleagues to maintain and develop this repertoire, is integral to a good formative assessment approach. Double questions, leading questions, rhetorical questions and closed questions (those looking for a unique correct answer) can discourage students from reflecting on the problem, or from revealing that they do not understand it. These kinds of questions can even inhibit learning and should usually be avoided.

Much more useful are open questions that require students to think about the problem and to find their own words to answer it. These might take the form of challenging (how /

why did you do that?), checking (do you know…?), uncovering thinking (can you explain this?), offering strategies (have you thought about….?), or re-assuring (are you happy with that?). Sometimes a 'devil's advocate' question (are you sure?) can be useful (see Swain *et al.*, 2006). In this way, teachers shift from being presenters of content to facilitators exploring ideas that the students are involved with. Students can be encouraged to think and talk more by the right kind of questioning and listening, and this is likely to produce useful outcomes in terms of knowledge about the students' understanding and their pre-conceptions, as well as time for the teacher to think about responsive strategies, while they listen to their students.

KEY POINTS

- Classrooms with lots of purposeful and focused talk are more likely to be rich learning environments than silent ones. Useful kinds of talk include dialogue between teacher and students and between students, questions from students and from the teacher, arguments and group discussion as part of collaborative tasks.

- One of the teacher's main roles is to build and sustain an atmosphere in the class that supports student engagement in challenging learning activities, including asking questions, expressing uncertainty, collaborative work with other students, and self- and peer-assessment.

- While careful lesson planning is vital, it is important that plans can adapt to students' responses and their varied understandings, misunderstandings and difficulties, as well as to their correct responses and insights. Students are more likely to be active agents of their own learning if they see that what they do and say makes a difference to what the teacher does.

- Classroom questioning by the teacher, and encouraging students to ask questions to further their learning, are critical elements of effective teaching. Some kinds of question support learning more than others.

- Teachers need to develop and extend their communication skills and practices, through discussions with colleagues and others and, ideally, through opportunities to take part in research. The way the teacher talks and behaves in the classroom is a central component of this atmosphere conducive to effective learning.

Providing constructive feedback through dialogue

There is powerful evidence that the most important element of the teaching and learning process, in terms of student achievement, is good oral and written feedback on students' performance, answers and responses to particular tasks (Fraser *et al.*, 1987; Black and Wiliam, 1998a). In contrast to transmission of content, and repetitive practice in the form of assignments or worksheet tasks at home or in the classroom, emphasis on feedback requires teachers to design classroom or homework activities that can generate evidence of students' understanding of relevant subject knowledge, and of their ability to use this knowledge in real-life situations.

Evidence for feedback can be produced by almost any activity, whether formal or informal, planned or accidental. This evidence can take the form of written assignments, worksheet tasks, or other materials produced by individuals or groups inside and outside formal sessions, It can also consist of the answers students give to oral questioning in the classroom, or even of their body language when confronted with a learning challenge. In addition, summative assessment activities such as formal tests, examinations, or other external assessment processes, even though this is not their primary purpose, also produce evidence which could in principle be used for feedback to students aiming to enhance learning.

This evidence is used by the teacher, often *in situ*, enabling them to offer feedback which:

- helps clarify what good performance is;

- facilitates the development of skills of self-assessment and reflection;

- provides students with high-quality information about the quality of their understanding or performance;

- encourages teacher and peer dialogue around learning;

- encourages positive motivation in learners;

- provides information to teachers to shape teaching.

(Adapted from Gibbs and Simpson, 2003.)

All teachers use feedback to a greater or lesser extent, but a formative approach urges teachers to embed it in their planning, to use it systematically in ways which promote learning and improve motivation. Research suggests that in order to be most beneficial, oral and written feedback should normally:

- focus on the task rather than the person's feelings or sense of self;

- be highly-focused, constructive and practical, including advice about how specific aspects of the work could be improved;

- avoid general statements of praise or criticism. (Praise given on its own, without specific advice about improving the work, can be frustrating to students and may not increase their motivation. One study found that learners only given praise or grades did no better than those who were given no feedback at all, and that the work of learners given only constructive advice improved considerably (Butler, 1998));

- be given as soon as possible: research suggests that oral feedback is more effective than written feedback;

- emphasise appropriate success criteria and relate to the learning objectives of the student(s);

- aim to develop the learners' own understanding of quality and ability to assess their own performance, whatever the subject and context, by drawing attention both to successful areas of work and to problems;

- reflect high expectations of the learner, and should avoid being patronising;

- not be quantified, though reference to appropriate level descriptors may be appropriate. (Giving grades or marks can demotivate students, especially those who are least confident, and particularly if the grades are made public and compared.);

- be part of an ongoing dialogue and continuous process of

assessment: the giving of feedback does not guarantee that students will pay attention to it – part of the teacher's role is to check whether their feedback is having an impact on the students' work.

Although feedback is normally seen as a one-to-one process between the teacher and an individual student, about a specific piece of work, if the task or activities concerned have been collaborative then group feedback may be appropriate. Feedback from the teacher is likely to make more sense and to have a greater impact if students have already assessed the work themselves in some way. If handled well, feedback can enhance trust, group cohesion and the motivation of the students involved.

Despite the obvious benefits and appeal of carefully designed feedback, research studies show that that much feedback in post-compulsory education raises student expectations of being coached to achieve each criterion, or of being given advice that they can translate easily and instrumentally into higher grades. As with other apparently formative techniques, feedback can end up as little more than instrumental and mechanistic pointers towards summative targets that don't really engage students in any meaningful learning (see for example Ecclestone 2010).

KEY POINTS

- Feedback has the potential to be the most important factor in student progression and achievement.

- Effective feedback is constructive and focused on how performance of learning tasks can be improved.

- Effective feedback focuses explicitly on success criteria, so that students know what they are trying to achieve, not just in terms of skills, but of fluency in performance.

- Giving feedback can be highly motivational, even if it is critical.

- Planning should be centrally focused on activities that produce information about the learners' performance and understanding to inform feedback.

- Feedback is an ongoing process, and is ideally integrated seamlessly into teaching and learning.

- As far as possible, feedback should focus specifically on tasks and progress not general 'ego' states, or feelings. Whilst important, praise and concern to reinforce or promote confidence can too often obscure the need for precise note of strengths and weaknesses on particular things.

Collaborative learning activities based on real-life problems and situations relevant to all the students

The most common model of teaching observed in ALLN classes in England consists of an introduction to a topic by the teacher to the whole group, followed by individual activities (see Derrick *et al.*, 2008). These usually take the form of students working through worksheets related to the topic, (often different students are working on different material) and being supported by the teacher periodically as s/he goes round the room, and as and when s/he is asked for help. There are good logistical reasons for this structure: it allows for students of varying levels of skill and confidence to be taught within the same group, and it allows for new students to join the group at any time.

However, collaborative discussions, tasks and activities, organised around conceptual obstacles, including disagreement and debate, rather than predominantly individual and more or less silent working, can have benefits for many students. Such approaches are likely to be even more effective with students who have not done well previously as a result of 'transmission-oriented' teaching they may have encountered before. For example, the NRDC Effective Practice studies in Reading, ESOL and Numeracy all in different ways suggest that more collaborative working in classes is likely to benefit learners. This is particularly clear in the context of learning ESOL, in which 'talk is work' (Spiegel and Sunderland, 2006; Roberts *et al.*, 2004). The benefits of collaborative writing include:

- helping learners to combine their strengths rather than to focus on their weaknesses;

- fostering a supportive and co-operative group that gives learners the security to take risks with their writing;

- providing opportunities for dialogue, and helping learners to anticipate potential readers' responses;

- making the process of revision more meaningful;

- promoting learner autonomy.

(Adapted from Grief, 2007.)

Working together on carefully-designed learning tasks can help students become clear about and articulate their own ideas, both about teaching, assessment and learning, and about the subject matter, and to compare and discuss them with others. They are then in a better position to reflect on these and perhaps to adapt them. Collaborative tasks require students to communicate with each other, and to 'try ideas out' with each other. A positive culture of co-operation and communication, planned for and encouraged by the teacher, promotes motivation, confidence, and autonomy, as well as enabling students to acquire knowledge about particular topics. Such a culture can also allow for disagreement and debate about relevant issues. In learning maths, for example, Swan (2007) argues that the teacher's role is in some sense to create conflicts and 'perturbations' with students conceptual frameworks, so that these frameworks can be adapted as part of learning. His research found that neither 'expository' or 'guided discovery' teaching approaches were as successful as what he calls the 'conflict discussion' style. He suggests that the most productive activities in this approach will:

- be focused on particular conceptual obstacles;

- be designed to focus on general, structural features, rather than aspects of specific tasks or numerical values;

- pose, and allow students to pose, questions that are challenging;

- encourage a variety of 'interpretations' to become explicit and to be compared and evaluated;

- involve questions being posed in such a way as creates a tension which needs to be resolved: for example getting students to solve a problem intuitively and then compare their answers with the results produced with a calculator;

- provide opportunities for feedback to each student on their particular interpretation;

- be followed by a whole-class discussion aiming to produce consensus;

- provide opportunities to consolidate what has been learned.

(Adapted from Swan 2007.)

KEY POINTS

- Organising learning through taking part in collaborative learning tasks, and using this work for self- and peer assessment, is likely to benefit many students, particularly those with less confidence.

- The tasks need to be planned carefully, with individual students in mind, and integrated into the overall scheme of work.

- How the teacher follows up such work, with questioning and feedback, is critical to its benefits being realised.

Developing learner autonomy, motivation and confidence through peer and self-assessment activities

Increased students' autonomy should be a central objective of teaching and learning in all education, and particularly in ALLN. Students need to be able to practise the skills and knowledge they acquire through their learning in real-life situations, whether this be at work, in their roles as citizens, parents and carers, and also in subsequent education and training situations. It is therefore important that teaching and learning goes beyond the ability to perform well in the artificial environment of the classroom. Students need to be able to use their new skills as confidently and fluently as possible once they no longer have the support of the class and the teacher. They need to develop the ability to perform and simultaneously to monitor their performance, and that of others they interrelate with, in the same way that we all do when we are driving a car: we get better at it with practice, until it becomes mostly routine. This applies equally to speaking and listening, reading and writing, and also to dealing with real-life situations and decisions of various kinds which require mathematical understanding, confidence and skills.

A formative assessment approach lays great emphasis on this aspect of teaching and learning, which is not easily assessed through the usual tests and paper-based examinations. It argues that we need to build self- and peer-assessment practice into more classroom work than in traditionally the case. This enables students to practise and develop their capacity to make critical, aesthetic and practical judgements of the quality and effectiveness of their developing skills and knowledge. Without these skills, what they learn will be de-contextualised and more difficult to transfer between different situations outside the classroom.

The focus of this type of assessment is on fluency and successful performance, the evaluation of which may, in part, be a matter of personal judgement or opinion. This fluency can only be developed through practice, and students may need to be provided with relevant conceptual tools, as well as practical collaborative experience of making, exchanging judgements of the quality of their own and others' work.

Unfortunately, the dominance of summative testing means that success criteria for 'passing' the official end-of-course assessment process are unlikely to be the same as success criteria for using the same skills effectively in everyday life situations. The test may require additional skills and knowledge not required in real life, and may ignore other skills and knowledge that are often needed to get by outside the world of education. This is to some extent inevitable, as no formal assessment can be perfect. Nevertheless, if we do not teach to go beyond the test and, instead, teach with a strong focus on real-life performance, we are very likely to be selling our students short.

Yet, while self-assessment and peer-assessment activities are crucial, relatively few ALLN teachers observed in research studies use these activities very much, and those that do tend not to integrate them into all aspects of the course. One reason for this is that many adult education teachers are nervous about challenging their learners, some of whom appear to lack the confidence to taking a more active and participatory role in learning. Some adults' attitudes to teaching, learning and assessment also reflect cultural barriers based on their previous experience of education. 'Traditional' transmission modes of teaching, in which students are seen largely as passive recipients, do not address the need to develop confidence outside the classroom. Instead, they assume that better performance in the class will always produce improved confidence and better performance in real life.

Addressing these barriers needs careful preparation, but can produce great benefits since improving confidence in their learning is a key aim of most adult students, who are generally highly-motivated to learn. A formative approach can help develop motivation, confidence and autonomy, but it needs teachers to create and sustain an atmosphere that is conducive to supporting students to take risks and get out of their comfort zones. Students need to be relaxed enough to ask questions when they don't understand, to be ready to make mistakes, and to have a go at self- and peer-assessment as part of their learning. Enabling many students to do this is often the most important (and difficult) job of the teacher in the early stages of a students' learning as an adult.

In the next section, among the case studies, is an example of a sequence of self- and peer-assessment activities organised over half a term's work in a low level ESOL class. As developing assessment skills and understanding, these activities also involve learning vocabulary, and improving speaking and listening skills. Here, we offer an example of a situation in a numeracy class where the group is divided into small groups, each working on this problem.

1. The final score in a hockey game was 2–1.

2. List the possible half-time scores.

3. How many possible scores are there?

4. Try this for other scores.

5. Write your results into a chart

6. Is there a pattern?

(Adapted slightly from NCETM, 2008)

After 15 minutes, each group presents their results to the whole group. Each group is encouraged to comment on other groups' findings and theories about the pattern involved. The exercise, structured in this way has at least four benefits, according to the teacher:

- it gets students used to 'challenging each other comfortably';

- it gets them involved in what may seem to be 'difficult' maths;

- it demonstrates that there is maths in all sorts of situations in life;

- it gives students practice in being able to describe a situation mathematically.

(NCETM 2008)

This exercise can also provide rich evidence for the teacher upon which to base further developmental questioning, and to give constructive feedback to individuals and to the group as a whole. It demonstrates well how different aspects of the formative assessment approach can all be seen in the same group of linked activities, and how turning serious learning activities into games involving lots of talk can often overcome the challenge felt by less-confident students.

As an introduction to peer-assessment within the group, students can be given model answers, both good and not so good, and asked to suggest ways in which they could be improved. This exercise could be arranged to follow one in which students had worked on developing their own list of appropriate assessment criteria, allowing them to use their list on a real piece of work. Groups of students can design questions on the relevant topic for the other groups, and then assess the answers given against both official and unofficial assessment criteria.

KEY POINTS

- Developing confidence in self- and peer-assessment in the use of ALLN skills is an essential element of being able to use those skills fluently and confidently in real-life situations outside the course.

- Self- and peer-assessment activities need to be carefully planned, and integrated into programmes of learning and schemes of work.

- It is often helpful to design activities as games involving lots of talk, and an element of competition.

Section 2

Case studies: Introduction

We offer three case study scenarios derived from recent research in ALLN classes. They are intended to illustrate ways in which formative assessment approaches can be designed and carried out in ALLN classes. They are not meant to be read as examples of perfect practice, but as models of practice that can be used for professional development discussions, and also adapted for use in other teachers' classrooms. We suggest that readers ask themselves:

- What is formative about this scenario?

- How could they be improved or adapted for my classes?

- How would I integrate this or similar activities into my scheme of work?

- How would my students benefit from this or similar activities in terms of learning and autonomy?

The section concludes with some ideas about continuous professional development for teachers organised on formative principles.

Scenario 1. ESOL: Self- and peer-assessment with Entry Level students

Ruth is a teacher working with a group of eight Entry 1 and Entry 2 ESOL students in an inner-city further education college. There are varying degrees of confidence in the group, some of them relaxed about participating in group activities, and others more reluctant to speak to the group as a whole, and tending to speak only to the teacher in one-to-one situations, or when asked a direct question.

The curriculum focus for the class is mostly on the speaking and listening sections of the Adult ESOL Curriculum standards. Ruth wants to incorporate simple self- and peer-assessment activities into learning activities built around making short spoken presentations to the group. In particular, she wants the students to engage in evaluation of their own and each others' presentations. These activities are planned to take place over several sessions, so that students get used to the ideas, words, and to working in a group. She is careful to ensure that each member of the group is involved in the activities, though this is difficult at times. If someone resists speaking to the whole group, she gets them to work with their neighbour. She continually reminds the students of the point of the whole exercise: to talk about what makes a good public speaking performance, so as to support their own performances for assessment purposes, and to improve their confidence. She also emphasises that the activity is meant to be constructive and supportive, and based on mutual trust and respect between the students.

She starts with an activity based around discussion of what makes a good public speaker, using examples from television such as politicians, TV presenters, and sports celebrities. The group produces a list of quality criteria, and

Ruth produces a series of learning activities based on the words involved.

These include such simple ideas as speaking loudly enough to be heard, speaking clearly, making it enjoyable for the listeners, interesting content, and correct use of English. She spends significant amounts of time on this activity. At times it is a struggle – one or two of the students are not used to participating in learning activities in this way. But even if the process doesn't go perfectly at all times, overall it does help the less confident students to participate more confidently, which Ruth sees as a crucial learning objective:

Presenting, discussing or even implementing imperfect strategies can be of great value as it forces the students to identify the criteria by which to plan and judge future assessments. How often does a teaching strategy work absolutely perfectly?

The planning and preparation of the students' presentations is another stage of this extended process. Ruth gives them simple templates to 'scaffold' their work, and allows sufficient time for revisions and reworking. Some work on individual presentations, and others do them in pairs.

The students' actual presentations are followed by the self- and peer-assessment stage. This starts with group discussion, followed by individual students making their personal assessments. The teacher organises simple record sheets on which students assess their own performance, and that of each of their peers, against the criteria already agreed by the group. They use a very simple classification system such as 'traffic lights': the point is not the actual results as much as the practical learning fostered by the process. She then adds her own assessments. The differences between these three distinct assessments are then discussed. Most students find that they have assessed themselves at a lower level than their peers' assessments of them.

Ruth's conclusions are that:

The learner input appears to lead to increased motivation. It's easy when teaching low-level groups to forget that they are sophisticated thinking people. The focus on trust and respect worked: at the beginning of the year some of them wouldn't listen to each other, but now they are all happily doing self- and peer-assessment. It doesn't all work perfectly every time, but I now make this kind of activity a central element of my teaching strategy. The fact that they are 'low level' learners only means that my preparation has to be more careful, not that they can't do it.

Scenario 2. Adult Numeracy: Collaborative learning tasks with Entry 2 and 3 students

Hassan is teaching a mixed group of twelve numeracy students working at Entry 2 and Entry 3 in a prison classroom. He wants to improve their fluency in the use of estimation in simple numerical calculations. He explains to the students that they are going to play a game that will help them get better at estimating. The game is called Target 100, and he divides the group into six pairs, each with a calculator. He gives them a Sheet 1 with the rules of the game on it, and a Sheet 2 for recording each game. He demonstrates the game twice, and then the whole class play it once together. Then they play against each other in their pairs. In the game, the first player keys any number into the calculator, and the second has to multiply this by another number, aiming to get as close to 100 as possible. The players then repeat this operation in turn, until one of them hits the target. As they play they record each turn of the game on Sheet 2.

When the pairs have played a few times, Hassan gets them to discuss possible strategies for playing well. He writes the following statements on the board and asks students to suggest possible multipliers, giving reasons.

$23 \times \ldots\ldots\ldots = 100$

$93 \times \ldots\ldots\ldots = 100$

$121 \times \ldots\ldots\ldots = 100$

$256 \times \ldots\ldots\ldots = 100$

The students start making suggestions for the multipliers:

'I think the first one is about 5, because 20 x 5 is 100.'

'I think it will be a bit less than 5, say 4.9, because 23 x 5 will be more than 100.'

'I think the second one should be 1.1 because it will be about a tenth as much again.'

In this way he encourages them to develop strategies for playing the game. He gets them to look back at the games they recorded and see if they can improve them. He asks them to write down ideas for playing the game well. Then the pairs play the game again, to see if the strategies they have identified make help them get to the target more quickly.

Then he gets them to play the game using division instead of multiplication.

The game exposes the common misconception that multiplication always makes numbers bigger and that division makes them smaller. Even when this becomes clear, some students make rather wild estimates, but they get better with practice. Hassan continually encourages them to try to identify rules for playing the game well, by asking questions such as:

'Why is that a good strategy?'

'Would that always work?'

'Do you agree with Donna's suggestion?'

'What is the difference between Donna's and Kieron's suggestions?'

'Is there always a strategy that is best, or could you have two equally good ones?'

When a 'rule' seems to have been generally agreed, he writes it on the board.

Towards the end of the session, he holds a whole group discussion to consider what had been learned about multiplying and dividing decimal numbers. He leads the discussion carefully, so that the following clear points are clarified for the whole group:

Multiplying a number by a number greater than 1 makes it larger

Multiplying a number by a number smaller than 1 makes it smaller

Multiplying a number by a half makes it half as big

Then they identify similar rules for division.

(Adapted from NRDC/*Maths4Life*, 2007.)

Scenario 3. Adult Literacy: 'Recycling'

An adult literacy group of eleven students at Entry Level 3 in an inner-city FE college are working on the topic of 'recycling'. This topic arose out of discussions following the delivery of leaflets and recycling bins from the local council on the estates and houses where they live. The students are working in three sub-groups, organised by the teacher in order to offer them differentiated activities.

The teacher, Maggie, is preparing the students to sit an externally set exam at the end of the term, which requires skills in skimming, scanning, reading for gist and accuracy in identifying information. As well as placing emphasis on reading for comprehension, she has also been introducing and familiarising the students with the meta-language involved in what they are doing. She wants them to be as well prepared as possible for the exam and to feel confident about their reading skills. She also wants to give them practice without having the pressure of time, encouraging them to read really closely and not just jump at the first answer. As part of her learning aims she is:

... trying to get them to think about and identify what clues they've used, how did they get that answer and not just that they go, that answer...

One aspect of the multiple-choice questions is that often two of the four questions are very similar, and the students need to pick up on the subtle differences between them. The group has done similar practice tests before but the students are still getting answers 'wrong'. Maggie hopes the activity will encourage the students to cross check and 'narrow down' key words and key ideas. She wants them to engage in discussion with each other about why one answer might be 'right' rather than another, and to talk to each other about why they had reached that conclusion.

In the session, there is lots of focus on language, on spelling, recapping and reviewing of skills and knowledge covered in previous sessions. Maggie encourages the students to be active in the class, to spend lots of time talking to each other about the work, to feed back information, to present their ideas verbally and in writing. There are large felt tip pens and pieces of coloured paper on the desks and students are encouraged to write on the white board. Maggie begins by eliciting from the group what they understand by the word 'recycling', which the students define in different ways, including *'using things again', 'turning things into something else that can be used'*. Next, Maggie asks the group to think about what questions they want to ask about recycling, using question words that they had looked at in a previous session. One student writes the question words down the side of the white board and Maggie suggests the students work in pairs or threes to make a list on their pieces of coloured paper of key words or brief information to answer the questions. This way, all the students get involved in the discussions and the whole group contributes to providing answers:

What?   Green bottles, clear bottles, cans, newspapers

Why?   Prevent pollution, save materials, save trees, clean the roads, make new things

When?   Things are used, broken or spoiled

Maggie has provided texts and differentiated sets of questions for each of the three small groups. She knows which students have problems with individual words, but are not 'stopped by the words', who can get the gist. Also the student who is a very able and quick reader, but can't pick out the detail to answer the questions accurately. She knows which students are dyslexic and which students prefer to work more on their own and she has taken this all into account in her planning of the materials and the groupings. One group has a recycling leaflet, one a simplified version of the leaflet, and the third has the leaflet plus an accompanying letter. The students read through the texts, helping each other and underlining words that they don't understand. Maggie sits with each group in turn, listening to their reading, checking their understanding and prompting exploratory talk. There is lots of discussion between the students directly about the text, about the meanings of words, about their different perceptions and understanding of what they are reading, as well as talking about what they personally do around recycling at home.

This way of working collaboratively is commented on by two of the students:

'I like the reading, I like it and if you don't read it properly – because some of the questions they are similar, if you don't look at it carefully, you'll miss the right one.'

'… something I don't know, then somebody knows, so everybody can give a view and we can work it out between us so I think it's good.'

As each group finishes reading and discussing, Maggie hands out the accompanying worksheets containing multiple-choice questions about the texts. She reminds them about the importance of really understanding what they have read and of checking the questions carefully before answering them. She encourages the students to talk to each other about what information they take from the texts to answer the questions, using the images and pictures as well as the words, to compare their answers and if they are different, try to find out why. The groups work collaboratively and help each other and one group (the most able readers) finishes the questions and engages in wider discussions about recycling.

Finally the students are encouraged to share some of their thoughts about this activity with each other. Which questions are easy? Which questions are more difficult? Why is this so?

On the basis of these discussions, Maggie decides to amend her lesson planned for the following day, in order to recap on some of this for some students, and for others to move on to questions that ask students to distinguish fact from opinion. She also would like to see if some of the students could set questions for each other about the texts.

Section 3

Formative approaches to Continuing Professional Development

Effective teacher training and CPD aims to provide teachers with new and enhanced subject knowledge, alongside the modelling of good practice in the classroom. It should therefore follow that messages emerging about effective teaching and formative assessment in the context of adult learning can also be applied to teacher training and CPD contexts. In this case the trainer (if there is one) takes the role of the teacher, and the teacher the role of student. These messages are likely to be even more important in the context of initial teacher training, where it is essential that the trainers model good practice in teaching and learning.

For CPD the formative assessment approach suggests the value of teachers undertaking small-scale action-research projects, ideally working with experts to identify meaningful professional problems and to use their own classroom as the laboratory for changing an aspect of their practice and then evaluating them formally and informally with colleagues and more broadly at conference workshops.

This model combines a number of aspects of a formative approach to learning: it is teacher-led, it is collaborative and sustainable, and it is practical and based in 'real work' situations. Crucially, however, just like students learning from an expert teacher, CPD requires some guidance and input from experts in the form of interventions and contributions in the form of academic articles or keynote speeches at conferences, any of which can stimulate developmental discussion and evaluation by groups of teacher colleagues.

Dylan Wiliam points out that teachers like opportunities to talk to each other about their work, and he sees the formative approach to CPD as starting with this and then formalising it slightly. He imagines groups of eight to ten colleagues, probably working in similar subject areas, meeting regularly to plan and evaluate classroom innovations or experiments undertaken by each member between meetings, in their classes. Meetings might take place twice-termly for two hours, and follow a strict agenda which would include verbal reports from each member on their activities since the last meeting, group discussions about how the activities went, a short 'input' element, which might be led by someone from another CPD group, and finally a section on planning the next round of experiments. Practical input and advice from ALLN experts and experienced researchers in the field can also support in-depth reflection and bring wider perspectives and knowledge to this process. Local or regional professional development centres (PDCs), teacher training networks and organisations like NIACE and the National Research and Development Centre for Adult Literacy, Language and Numeracy (NRDC) are all sources of potential information and support for CPD.

The kinds of innovations teachers might try out might include using more self- and peer-assessment as part of their teaching, or new approaches to classroom questioning, or on how to make feedback more effective. 'Teacher learning communities' (Wiliam, 2007) like this have been piloted in the schools sector and found to be effective in making a difference to teachers' classroom practice. This approach to teacher development aims at 'a change in understanding rather than merely a superficial change in teaching techniques…teachers must have time to reflect and to adjust their teaching to take on new practices. Professional development activities are therefore best spread out over time, with opportunities for trying out new assessment ideas between sessions.' (Gardner *et al.*, 2008).

Possible classroom innovations for evaluation by teachers:

- new approaches to questioning in class;

- students developing their own assessment criteria for simple presentations made by members of the group, or short pieces of writing on specific topics;

- students assessing their own work against agreed assessment criteria;

- students creating their own examination questions;

- separate groups of students discussing how to approach solutions to given practical problems, and then comparing and evaluating each other's results;

- new approaches to giving feedback during class teaching;

- increasing the amount of student talk during classes;

- engaging in observations of each other's teaching and giving feedback on them.

Possible development activities during the teacher learning community meetings:

- discussion of the *Mathematics Matters* Principles that Guide Teaching (see Appendix 1);

- discussion of an agreed research paper that everyone has read in advance;

- evaluation of a conference members have all attended;

- cascading of insights from a conference workshop that one member has attended;

- discussion of a new policy document affecting teaching and learning;

- a teaching clinic: one member describes a problem in their class, others contribute ideas for addressing it;

- discussion of observations of each other's teaching, quality criteria and feedback.

Section 4

Resources and more information

Geoff Petty's website, full of good ideas and resources for teachers: **www.geoffpetty.com**

The Assessment Reform Group (ARG):
http://www.assessment-reform-group.org/publications.html

Teaching, learning and assessment for adults: improving foundation skills. A report and papers from a study by the OECD:
http://www.oecd.org/document/42/0,3343,en_2649_35845581_40026026_1_1_1_1,00.html

Annotated references and further reading

Research findings on improving teaching and learning

ARG (2002): Research-*based principles of assessment for learning to guide classroom practice* (London: Assessment Reform Group).

This leaflet/poster presents and briefly discusses ten principles of assessment for learning, based on research evidence. It can be downloaded at:
www.assessment-reform-group.org/publications.html

Black, P and Wiliam, D (1998a): 'Assessment and classroom learning: Principles, policy and practice', *Assessment in Education* 5(1) pp. 1–78.

This closely-argued paper reports on the findings of a meta-review of over 120 research studies on classroom formative assessment. It shows that innovations designed to strengthen frequent feedback to students on classroom tasks and activities 'yield substantial learning gains'. It includes detailed discussions of the perceptions of students and their role in self-assessment, of the strategies used by teachers, and on the nature of feedback.

Black, P and Wiliam, D (1998b): *Inside the black box: Raising standards through classroom assessment.* London: NfER Nelson.

This well-known pamphlet is a brief and accessible introduction to the concept of formative assessment in theory and practice, based on Black and Wiliam's major research paper on assessment and classroom learning. Its main focus is on teaching and learning in schools, but its discussion is highly relevant to post-compulsory contexts.

Boud, D (2000): 'Sustainable assessment: rethinking assessment for the learning society', *Studies in Continuing Education*, 22(2) pp. 151–167.

Boud argues that assessment practices tend not to equip students well for the processes of effective learning in a learning society. He proposes that the purposes of assessment should be extended to include the preparation of students for sustainable assessment, that is, the abilities required to undertake activities that necessarily accompany learning throughout life in formal and informal settings. He argues that this approach will help meet the specific and immediate goals of any particular course as well as establishing a basis for students to undertake their own assessment activities in the future.

Butler, R (1998): 'Enhancing and undermining intrinsic motivation: the effects of task-involving and ego-involving evaluation on interest and performance', *British Journal of Educational Psychology*, 58, pp. 1–14.

This study was designed to test the hypothesis that intrinsic motivation will be differentially affected by task-involving and ego-involving evaluation, and that provision of both kinds of evaluation will promote ego-involvement rather than task-involvement. It found that interest and performance were highest after evaluative comments focused on tasks, both when further comments were anticipated and when they were not. Grades and grades plus comments had similar and generally undermining effects on both interest and performance, although higher achievers who received grades maintained high interest when further grades were anticipated. The paper discusses these results in terms of the distinction it makes between task and ego-involvement and their connection with intrinsically-motivated activity.

Condelli, L, Wrigley, H S, Yoon, K, Seburn, M, and Cronen, S (2003): *'What Works' study for Adult ESL literacy students.* Washington DC: US Department of Education.

This study aimed to identify ways in which adult ESL programmes can provide effective instruction to improve the English language and literacy skills of students, by examining the effectiveness of different types of instruction, and by linking 'educational inputs', such as teaching strategies, with 'educational outcomes', including increases in test scores, for ESL literacy students. The study was designed to inform improvements in instruction and programme design.

The project's key findings on instructional practices were:

- 'Bringing in the outside' – in classes where teachers made connections to the 'outside' or real world, students had more growth in reading basic skills development.

- Use of the students' native language for clarification – in classes where teachers used students' native language for clarification during instruction, students had faster growth in reading comprehension and oral communication skills.
- Varied practice and interaction strategy – where the teacher taught concepts in a variety of modalities and allowed student interaction, students had faster growth in oral communication skills.
- Emphasis on oral communication – where the teacher explicitly emphasised oral English communication skills in instruction, students had more growth in this area.

Other key findings were that longer scheduled classes produced more growth in reading comprehension and oral communication skills, but less growth in basic reading skills; that students that attended a higher proportion of scheduled time (in hours) had more growth in reading comprehension and oral communication skills; that students with more years of education and higher incoming English language and literacy skills had more growth in skills, though the effect of years of schooling was limited to growth in basic reading skills development; and that younger students developed basic reading and English oral communication skills faster than older students.

Davies, J and Ecclestone, K (2009): ' "Straitjacket" or "springboard" for sustainable learning? The implications of formative assessment practices in vocational educational learning cultures', *Curriculum*, 19(2), pp. 71–86.

This paper reports on findings from The Improving Formative Assessment Project (IFA). Focusing mainly on vocational learning programmes in post-compulsory learning contexts, it evaluates the influence of learning cultures on how far formative assessment is practised in the 'letter' or in the 'spirit', and what the consequences are for the kind of learning that takes place. This paper offers provisional answers to two closely related questions: Why do some learning cultures foster formative assessment that leads to instrumental learning while others foster formative assessment designed for sustainable learning? When is the letter of formative assessment a springboard for the spirit of it, and therefore for sustainable learning, and when does it remain a straitjacket?

Derrick, J and Ecclestone, K (2008): 'English-language Literature Review', in *Teaching, Learning and Assessment for Adults: Improving Foundation Skills*. Paris: OECD Publishing. Accessed 8 May 2009 at **http://dx.doi.org/10.1787/172251338713**

This review surveys 99 publications on effective pedagogy, mostly focused on adult foundation students. Its discussion is organised around the headings of: developing an atmosphere and culture conducive to learning; dialogue between teachers and learners; peer- and self-assessment; learners' understanding of assessment and the language of assessment; feedback and marking of work; questioning and checking learning; planning and differentiation; improving motivation, confidence, autonomy and citizenship; using different types of assessment formatively; and practising assessment: learning for the future. The review concludes with a chapter summarising its messages for teachers, and with an annotated list of the texts surveyed.

Derrick, J, Gawn, J and Ecclestone, K (2008): 'Evaluating the "spirit" and "letter" of formative assessment in the learning cultures of part-time adult literacy and numeracy classes', *Research in Post-Compulsory Education*, 13 (2), pp. 173–184.

This paper reports on findings from The Improving Formative Assessment Project (IFA), and uses a socio-cultural approach to explore the relationship between formative assessment practices and 'learning cultures' in part-time adult literacy, numeracy and ESOL classes. Analysing fieldwork in six literacy and numeracy classes within two different organisations, it discusses whether classroom practices exemplify the 'letter' or the 'spirit' of formative assessment, and suggests ways in which formative assessment practices that encourage sustainable learning can be better supported in this type of learning context.

Ecclestone, K. (2010): *Transforming formative assessment in lifelong learning.* Chichester: Open University Press

Drawing on extensive data from an in-depth funded research project, this book discusses how factors in different 'learning cultures' can make any formative assessment 'method' or approach highly instrumental or genuinely educational and transforming. It shows how much formative assessment in further and adult education is presented in the right rhetoric, and sounds formative, but in practice, can be little more than coaching to the targets. The book reiterates and updates current thinking on what formative assessment is, and is not, and demonstrates how learning cultures in vocational education and adult literacy, language and numeracy programmes can shape formative assessment in particular ways. The book highlights ways in which teachers and institutional managers can resist pressures to use formative assessment narrowly and instrumentally.

Fielding, M, Bragg, S, Craig, J, Cunningham, I, Eraut, M, Gillinson, S, Horne, M, Robinson, C and Thorp, J (2005): *Factors Influencing the Transfer of Good Practice.* Research Brief RB615. London DfES.

This research report from the DfES recommends that teacher development should be organised around ongoing teacher-led discussion and evaluation of their work in a process it calls 'joint practice development', rather than the government's preference for transfer of 'best practice'. The teachers surveyed by the researchers valued professional learning that was a genuine shared dialogue over time, in which they reflected and acted upon individual and collective experiences of teaching. They wanted to be actively engaged in their CPD, not to be passive recipients of external ideas of 'best practice'.

Fraser, B, Wahlberg, H, Welch, W and Hattie, J (1987): 'Identifying the salient facets of a model of student learning: a synthesis of meta-analyses', *International Journal of Educational Research*, Vol 11, pp. 187–212.

This paper is one of six chapters making up a long monograph which aims to identify consistent and powerful predictors of student learning so that recommendations can be made for improving the educational productivity of schools. The paper discusses issues in the major models of student learning in the literature and presents a model which retains the salient features of these models. It is based on a synthesis of 134 meta-analyses of achievement outcomes, and 92 meta-analyses of attitude outcomes, to identify which factors make the most difference to both types of outcome. It finds that learning is most strongly dependent on the student aptitudinal variables of:

(1) ability,

(2) development or age, and

(3) motivation;

the instructional variables of

(4) quantity of instruction, and

(5) quality of instruction;

and the environmental variables of

(6) home environment,

(7) classroom environment,

(8) peer group environment, and

(9) mass media environment.

The paper provides a highly detailed comparative correlation of each of these factors with learning.

Gardner, J, Harlen, W, Hayward, L and Stobart, G (2008): *Changing Assessment Practice – Process, Principles and Standards.* Assessment Reform Group.

This pamphlet looks at the most effective approaches to generating and sustaining improved assessment practices in classrooms, based on a study of selected projects involving innovative assessment practice, and a series of expert seminars and interviews. It concludes that sustainable development requires careful design, thorough planning and implementation, commitment from teachers, managers, researchers, teacher educators and policymakers, and the involvement of learners too. It concludes with a set of principles and standards describing widely-held conceptions of good practice in assessment, for classrooms, management teams, local and national inspection, and for policy formulation.

Gibbs, G and Simpson, C (2003): *Does your Assessment Support your Students' Learning?* Centre for Higher Education Practice Open University. Accessed 8 May 2009 at **http://isis.ku.dk/kurser/blob.aspx?feltid=157744**

Much evaluation of teaching focuses on what teachers do in class. This article focuses on the evaluation of assessment arrangements and the way they affect student learning out of class. It is assumed that assessment has an overwhelming influence on what, how and how much students study. The article proposes a set of 'conditions under which assessment supports learning' and justifies these with reference to theory, empirical evidence and practical experience. These conditions are offered as a framework for teachers to review the effectiveness of their own assessment practice.

Looney, J (2008): *Teaching, Learning and Assessment for Adults: Improving Foundation Skills*. Paris: OECD Publishing.

This report is based on a study of teaching, learning and assessment practices in adult foundation learning contexts in seven countries in Europe and America, including detailed case studies, literature reviews in four language traditions, and an overview of policies and programmes for adult learners of literacy, numeracy and language. It identifies seven interrelated principles, which it proposes should serve as a broad framework for strengthening policy and practice: promoting active debate on the nature of teaching, learning and assessment; strengthening professionalism; balancing structure and flexibility; strengthening learner-centred approaches; diversifying approaches to assessment for accountability; devoting the resources required; and strengthening the knowledge-base.

Pickering, J (2007): 'Teachers' professional development – Not whether or what, but how', in *New Designs for Teachers' Professional Learning*, ed J Pickering, C Daly, N Pachler. London: Institute of Education.

Reder, S (1994): 'Practice engagement theory – a socio-cultural approach to literacy across languages and cultures', in *Literacy across languages and cultures*, ed. Ferdman, B,

Weber, R and Ramirez, R. Albany: State University of New York Press, pp. 33–74.

This paper takes a social psychological perspective, describing literacy as a social and cultural process comprising a set of culturally-defined practices. It summarises research showing how literacy practices vary across cultural groups within a society. Reder argues for the importance of what he calls 'practice-engagement theory', which proposes that teachers and programmes need to understand how literacy practices develop through collaborative activity, that 'participation structures' are contexts for literacy development, that social meanings shape literacy development, and that literacy develops primarily through acquisition and extension of existing practices, rather than through the learning of 'new' ones. In particular, practice engagement theory provides accounts for how fluency in literacy practices can be developed without formal instruction. It follows from this that formal instruction needs firstly to be aligned as far as possible to the specific literacy practices that individual learners' are familiar with already, and secondly, to try to build learning on these practice-specific contexts rather than separately from them.

Sadler, R (1989): 'Formative assessment and the design of instructional systems', *Instructional Science*, Vol 18, pp. 119–144.

This article discusses the nature and function of formative assessment in the development of students' expertise for evaluating the quality of their own work. It argues that for students to be able to improve, they must develop the capacity to monitor the quality of their own work while they are doing it. This in turn requires that students possess an appreciation of what high-quality work is, that they have the evaluative skill necessary for them to compare with some objectivity the quality of the work they are producing in relation to the higher standard, and that they develop a store of tactics or moves that can be drawn upon to modify their own work. The paper argues that these skills can be developed by providing direct authentic evaluative experience for students.

Swain, J, Griffiths, G and Stone, R (2006): 'Integrating formative/diagnostic assessment techniques into teachers' routine practice in adult numeracy', *Research and Practice in Adult Literacy (RaPAL) Journal* No 59, pp. 17–20.

This paper reports on a study of teachers' ability to assess the mathematical understanding of learners, and better integrate formative assessment into their routine practice. Data was collected by observations of questioning by six teachers, through peer observations, in depth interviews, reflective journals, and four group review sessions, with the teachers as participants. The study offers a typology for questioning, and found that teachers' practice and understanding of learning was improved by the focus on questioning. It also found improved levels of motivation in both teachers and learners.

Swan, M (2006): *Collaborative learning in mathematics: a challenge to our beliefs and practices.* Leicester: NIACE/NRDC.

This book begins with an account of what we now know about learning situations in mathematics, drawing on research and development work conducted over 25 years. It considers research-based principles for effective teaching and learning, and reports on trials of these approaches in the classroom. It describes the impact of these approaches have had on the professional development of more than 40 teachers, in terms of changes to their beliefs and practices, and the resulting effects on their students' learning. Analysis of these trials produces new theoretical insights into both the design of learning activities and into approaches to the initial and Continuing Professional Development of all teachers of mathematics. The major focus of the various research projects reported on is GCSE learning for low-achieving students ('retake' classes in particular) and their teachers. It concludes that a more student-centred, collaborative approach to learning, where discussion and reflection are central, will be more effective that the traditional transmission approach, with regard to the development of student understanding of, and attitudes towards learning, mathematics. It suggests that activities for learning should be designed so as to: focus on particular conceptual obstacles; focus on general, structural features rather than task-specific features; pose, or allow students to pose, significant and challenging questions; encourage a variety of interpretations; create tensions that require resolution, through careful juxtaposition of experiences; provide meaningful feedback to the student on his or her interpretations; be followed by some form of whole-class discussion in which new ideas and concepts are made explicit and institutionalised; allow 'consolidation' of what has been learned through the application of the students' constructed concepts. Swan concludes by saying that though this approach might appear to take more time than traditional transmission methods, 'it will result in student learning and, ultimately, a more enjoyable experience for all concerned.'

Practitioner guidance

Black, P, Harrison, C, Lee, C, Marshall, B and Wiliam, D (2003): *Assessment for learning: putting it into practice.* Buckingham: Open University Press.

This book is based on a two-year project involving 36 teachers in schools in Medway and Oxfordshire. It reviews the research background of Assessment for Learning and of the project itself, and has chapters which examine the assessment practices teachers in the project found fruitful, and which look at the implications of these for theoretical models of learning. Later chapters discuss the problems teachers encountered in implementing the new practices in their classrooms, and give guidance for managers and policymakers in promoting and supporting improvements in practice.

Burton, M (2007): *Reading: Developing Adult Teaching and Learning, a practitioner guide.* Leicester: NIACE/NRDC.

One of a series of practitioner guides to good practice in the fields of adult language literacy and numeracy teaching and learning. Each guide in the series aims to update teachers on research and to encourage them to reflect on their practice. Principles of good practice are illustrated by clear and relevant case studies from current research, and pointers to further reading are provided. All the guides are available to download from:
http://www.nrdc.org.uk/content.asp?CategoryID=502

Collard, P, Carpenter, L and Sampson, M (Basic Skills Agency) (2007): *Tools for Staff Development: Module 2: Assessment for Learning.* Leicester: NIACE.

This module supports teachers in making the best use of the outcomes of assessment so that learners learn effectively. Putting the learner at the heart of the teaching and learning process, this module examines practical ideas for how to:

• make the purpose of assessment clear to learners;

• set targets that learners can understand;

• develop consistent approaches to marking and oral and written feedback;
• use questioning strategies to support learning.

The materials are grounded in research and theory but provide very practical experience and activities that can be applied immediately in the classroom in a wide range of adult and post-16 contexts and settings.

Cooke, M and Roberts, C (2007): *ESOL: Developing Adult Teaching and Learning, a practitioner guide.* Leicester: NIACE/NRDC.

One of a series of practitioner guides to good practice in the fields of adult language literacy and numeracy teaching and learning. Each guide in the series aims to update teachers on research and to encourage them to reflect on their practice. Principles of good practice are illustrated by clear and relevant case studies from current research, and pointers to further reading are provided. All the guides are available to download from:
http://www.nrdc.org.uk/content.asp?CategoryID=502

Grief, S (2007): *Collaborative writing.* London: NRDC.

This short leaflet reports on the findings of a development project that was part of the NRDC Effective Practice study in writing. It looks at a range of collaborative writing activities, the responses of teachers and learners to these activities, the value of these activities in terms' of learners' writing, the role of the teacher in supporting collaborative writing, the role of resources, and the wider benefits for learners of collaborative activities. The leaflet can be downloaded from:
http://www.nrdc.org.uk/publications_details.asp?ID=110

Grief, S, Chatterton, J (2007): *Writing: Developing Adult Teaching and Learning, a practitioner guide.* Leicester: NIACE/NRDC.

One of a series of practitioner guides to good practice in the fields of adult language literacy and numeracy teaching and learning. Each guide in the series aims to update teachers on research and to encourage them to reflect on their practice. Principles of good practice are illustrated by clear and relevant case studies from current research, and pointers to further reading are provided. All the guides are available to download from:
http://www.nrdc.org.uk/content.asp?CategoryID=502

NCETM (2008): *Mathematics Matters.* London: National Centre for Excellence in the Teaching of Mathematics.

This booklet reports on a consultation undertaken by NCETM which aimed to establish an agreed set of valued learning outcomes and an agreed set of principles, grounded in evidence, underpinning the learning and teaching of mathematics. It presents five outcomes it suggests are sought by all mathematics teaching and learning, and 11 principles for informing the best teaching. It also identifies key barriers to progress in learning, and makes four broad recommendations for moving forward.

NRDC/Maths4Life (2007): *Thinking Through Mathematics: Strategies for teaching and learning.* London: NRDC/Maths4Life.

This pack was produced by Maths4Life, part of the Skills for Life programme and funded by the DfES. It provides research-based principles of effective teaching that underpin the Maths4Life project, 7 collaborative professional development sessions, 30 exemplar teaching and learning sessions on mathematical topics, a DVD video showing teachers using Maths4Life sessions and a CD ROM. The pack argues that all learners are capable of discussing and explaining ideas, challenging and teaching one another, creating and solving each other's questions, and working collaboratively to share methods and results.

QIA (2008a): *Guidance for assessment and learning 5: assessment for learning.* Skills for Life Improvement Programme. London: The Quality Improvement Agency.

This is one of a series of 5 Assessment and Learning booklets published by the Quality Improvement Agency as part of the Skills for Life Improvement Programme. It is available to download at:
http://sflip.excellencegateway.org.uk/pdf/4.2sflguidance_5.pdf

QIA (2008b): *Supporting Skills for Life learners to Stick with it! A guide for managers, practitioners and learners.* London: The Quality Improvement Agency.

This guide is based on the findings of the QIA-funded research project on Progression, Persistence and Achievement. It includes resources for learners, practitioners, curriculum managers and senior managers. It is available to download at
http://www.excellencegateway.org.uk/page.aspx?o=164919

Spiegel, M and Sunderland, H (2006): Teaching basic literacy to ESOL learners: a teachers' guide. London: London Language and Literacy Unit (LLU+), London Southbank University.

This is a comprehensive guide to the teaching of literacy to ESOL learners, that treats classroom assessment as integral to teaching and learning.

Swain, J, Newmarch, B and Gormley, O (2007): *Numeracy: Developing Adult Teaching and Learning, a practitioner guide.* Leicester: NIACE/NRDC.

One of a series of practitioner guides to good practice in the fields of adult language literacy and numeracy teaching and learning. Each guide in the series aims to update teachers on research and to encourage them to reflect on their practice. Principles of good practice are illustrated by clear and relevant case studies from current research, and pointers to further reading are provided. All the guides are available to download from:
http://www.nrdc.org.uk/content.asp?CategoryID=502

Learners

Appleby, Y (2008): *Bridges into learning for adults who find provision hard to reach: a practitioner guide.* Leicester: NIACE/NRDC.

One of a series of practitioner guides to good practice in the fields of adult language literacy and numeracy teaching and learning. Each guide in the series aims to update teachers on research and to encourage them to reflect on their practice. Principles of good practice are illustrated by clear and relevant case studies from current research, and pointers to further reading are provided. All the guides are available to download from:
http://www.nrdc.org.uk/content.asp?CategoryID=502

Appleby, Y and Barton, D (2008): *Responding to other people's lives.* Leicester: NIACE/NRDC.

One of a series of practitioner guides to good practice in the fields of adult language literacy and numeracy teaching and learning. Each guide in the series aims to update teachers on research and to encourage them to reflect on their practice. Principles of good practice are illustrated by clear and relevant case studies from current research, and pointers to further reading are provided. All the guides are available to download from:
http://www.nrdc.org.uk/content.asp?CategoryID=502

Roberts, C, Baynham, M, Shrubshall, P, Barton, D, Chopra, P, Cooke, M, Hodge, R, Pitt, K, Schellekens, P, Wallace, C and Whitfield, S (2004): *English for Speakers of Other Languages (ESOL) – case studies of provision, learners' needs and resources.* London: NRDC.

This report describes research which aimed to examine teaching in a wide variety of adult ESOL classes, and to establish some of the distinctive features of ESOL learners and provision so as to inform literacy and numeracy research. Its key findings were:

- Individualised teaching and learning may not support the needs of adult ESOL learners: talk is work in the ESOL classroom and the most significant mode of learning for ESOL learners is through group interaction.
- Effective teachers of ESOL employ a series of measures to support the needs of ESOL learners in the classroom.
- Most ESOL teachers juggle a variety of roles as well as teaching in relation to support for asylum seekers and refugees: they need more specialist knowledge and institutional support for these roles.
- The use of everyday, culturally specific situations to contextualise mathematics problem may act as a barrier to attainment by ESOL learners in numeracy classes.
- Teachers need to use strategies to encourage the use of learners' other languages within the teaching and learning of English.
- It may be that the involvement of learners in planning and reviewing of their learning through individual learning plans is not meaningful, as language learners appear unable to reflect on and predict their language development, even when they have an advanced level of English.

Teacher development

Atkinson, T, Claxton, G eds (2000): *The Intuitive Practitioner: on the value of not always knowing what one is doing.* Maidenhead: Open University Press.

This collection of papers maintains that much of the time, experienced professionals cannot comprehensively explain what they are doing, and yet discussion of professional development and practice takes for granted that completely conscious apprehension and rational analysis of practice are the norm. The book argues that intuition plays a central role in the development of professional practice and expertise, and explores the dynamic relationship between reason and intuition in the context of professional practice, mostly focusing on the professional world of the teacher. It includes discussions of the development of intuitive skills, the role of intuition in mentoring, complex decision-making in the classroom, assessment and intuition, and a critical overview of the concept of the intuitive practitioner.

Schön, D (1987): *Educating the Reflective Practitioner.* San Francisco: Jossey Bass.

This book starts with the observation that skilful professional practice often depends less on factual knowledge or rigid decision-making models than on the capacity to reflect before taking action in cases where established theories do not apply. Most training does not reflect this, and so fails to equip future professionals with the skills they need to deal with difficult problems of the real world. Schön argues that professional education should be centred on enhancing the practitioner's ability for 'reflection-in-action', that is, learning by doing and developing the capacity for continued learning and problem solving throughout the professional's career.

Wiliam, D (2007): 'Content then process: teacher learning communities in the service of formative assessment', in *Ahead of the curve: the power of assessment to transform teaching and learning,* ed. Reeves, D. Bloomington, Indiana: Solution Tree.

The argument of this chapter is that to raise student achievement, the usual models of teacher professional development will not be sufficient. Research shows that the most effective way to raise student achievement is to improve the quality of the teachers, and the only practical way to do this is to improve the teachers already working in schools and colleges. The paper argues that taking account of both costs and benefits of possible reforms reveals that helping teachers develop minute-by-minute and day-by-day formative assessment practices is more cost-effective than anything else. It suggests that changing the way all teachers work can't be done effectively through summer workshops or one-day in-service programmes. Rather it requires the formation of building-based 'professional learning communities' in which teachers holds each other accountable, and provides mutual support.

Impact of policy on effective teaching and learning

Derrick, J, Merrifield, J, Ecclestone, K (2007): 'A balancing act? The English and Welsh model of assessment in adult basic education', in *Assessment Practices in Adult Basic Education*, ed. Campbell, P. Edmonton: Canadian Adult Literacy Secretariat/Grass Roots Press.

This paper argues that, at least in relation to the UK government's *Skills for Life* strategy, the short-term needs of policymakers, funders and inspectors are different to those of teachers and learners. After an outline of the main features of the policy, the paper looks at the methods used and the difficulties experienced by various government agencies in evaluating the strategy's effectiveness and value for money, and argues that these methods have begun to damage effective teaching and learning. In particular, it is suggested that they inhibit the use of classroom assessment by teachers. The paper ends by discussing possibilities for improving the Skills for Life approach to assessment, and concludes that the possibility of a balance being achieved between the needs of learners and those of policymakers depends on the underlying theory of learning held by policy.

Harlen, W and Deakin Crick, R (2002): 'A systematic review of the impact of summative assessment and tests on students' motivation for learning', *Research Evidence in Education Library*, Issue 1. London: Institute of Education EPP.I-Centre review (version 1.1).

This systematic review aimed to identify the impact of summative assessment and testing on students' motivation for learning. The study found: that after the introduction of national curriculum tests in England low-achieving pupils had lower self-esteem than higher-achieving students; before the tests, there had been no correlation between self-esteem and achievement; that a strong emphasis on testing produces students with a strong extrinsic orientation towards grades and social status, i.e. a motivation towards performance rather than learning goals; that interest and effort are increased in classrooms which encourage self-regulated learning by providing students with an element of choice, control over challenge and opportunities to work collaboratively; and feedback that is ego-involving rather than task-involving is associated with an orientation to performance goals.

Torrance, H, Colley, H, Garratt, D, Jarvis, J, Piper, H, Ecclestone, K and James, D (2005): *The Impact of Different Modes of Assessment on Achievement and Progress in the Learning and Skills Sector*. London: Learning and Skills Development Agency.

This paper reports on research investigating whether or not, and if so how, use of different assessment methods makes a difference to learner achievement and progress in the learning and skills sector. It identifies an enduring divide between academic and vocational tracks and the different methods of assessment employed in those tracks. Overall the study finds that assessment methods per se do not directly affect learners' choice of award or likelihood of success, but the association of certain awards with methods which employ extensive writing (coursework, exam essays, etc) does. It discusses the increasing demand for transparency in assessment, but notes that while this can have benefits for learners, 'transparency encourages instrumentalism', and has led to a movement from what has been characterised as assessment *of* learning, through the currently popular idea of assessment *for* learning, to *assessment as learning*, 'where assessment procedures and practices may come completely to dominate the learning experience, and *criteria compliance* comes to replace learning.'

Appendix: Principles that guide teaching

(Adapted slightly from Mathematics Matters, NCETM 2008)

Teaching is more effective when …

1. It builds on the knowledge learners already have.

2. It exposes and discusses common misconceptions and other surprising phenomena.

3. It uses higher order questions.

4. It makes appropriate use of whole class interactive teaching, individual work and co-operative small group work.

5. It encourages reasoning rather than 'answer getting'.

6. It uses rich, collaborative tasks.

7. It creates connections between topics, both within and beyond the subject and with the real world.

8. It uses resources, including technology, in creative and appropriate ways.

9. It confronts difficulties rather than seeking to avoid or pre-empt them.

10. It develops the language of the subject through communicative activities.

11. It recognises both what has been learned and also how it has been learned.

Some unhelpful principles

1. Learn how to do it first – understanding will come later.

2. Repetition will improve understanding.

3. There is a 'best way' to teach, an 'optimal sequence' for learning, a 'right way' to tackle each task.

4. Explain clearly how to do the task before you give it to your class. Learning must be preceded by instruction.

5. Tell the class your lesson objectives at the beginning of each lesson.

6. Make sure your lesson has three parts.

7. Plan the plenary discussion very carefully and stick to your plan.

8. Cover the syllabus, even if this means hurrying through some parts.

9. Keep emphasising presentation and neatness.

10. Knowing the answer is important.

11. Keep learners busy. Learners go off-task if they talk.

12. Don't confuse learners by showing them incorrect methods.

13. Use technology whenever you can.